758.1

This b

LOOKING AT PAINTINGS

Landscapes

When the Mountains Meet the Mist, 1973
Diana Kan, American, born 1927

LOOKING AT PAINTINGS

Landscapes

Peggy Roalf

Series Editor
Jacques Lowe

Designer
Amy Hill

Belitha Press
London

THE ADORATION OF THE SHEPHERDS, about 1505–10
Giorgione da Castelfranco, Italian (1475/7–1510), 87.5 x 107 cm

Giorgione was inspired by the light in Castelfranco, the hill town where he was born. His observations of nature led him to invent a new painting method that was revolutionary at the time.

Painting without outlines

In the sixteenth century, artists were taught to make detailed drawings of every aspect of their subject before painting it. The use of colour was considered less important than an artist's ability to

Giorgione made this nativity scene look like a **contemporary** *event by setting it in the country-side where he had lived as a child.*

draw. But Giorgione worked in colour from the beginning. He had noticed that objects in nature do not have outlines and so created a feeling of light, air, and space by building up shades of colour without outlines.

Giorgione leads us on a circular walk into the landscape by painting curved and vertical shapes. He painted the lake as three flattened ovals that become smaller in size as they go into the background. A little path curves back from the shore towards the hillside beyond. The geometric lines of the golden tower, lakeside villa and ruined castle follow the circular path of Giorgione's design from the foreground to the horizon. With touches of red, Giorgione warmed the golden **tones** in the landscape to capture the beautiful light of the Venetian countryside.

Looking at Paintings

Landscapes

Peggy Roalf

Series Editor
Jacques Lowe

Designer
Amy Hill

Belitha Press
London

A
JACQUES LOWE
VISUAL ARTS PROJECTS
BOOK

First published in the United States by Hyperion Books for Children

Printed in Italy

First published in 1994 in the United Kingdom by

Belitha Press Ltd

31 Newington Green, London, N16 9PU

Cataloguing-in-print data available from the British Library

ISBN 1 85561 317 4

Priginal design concept by Amy Hill

UK Editor: Jill Laidlaw

Contents

To John Gundelfinger, with love

Introduction

LOOKING AT PAINTINGS is a series of books about understanding what great artists see when they paint. Painters have created landscapes for thousands of years, for many different reasons.

Two thousand years ago, a Roman artist painted landscape **murals** in country villas near Pompeii (page 9). These works of art show the luxury and wealth which was buried under molten lava when Mount Vesuvius erupted in AD 79. When Pompeii was unearthed by **archaeologists** in 1748, these murals captured the public's imagination with their great beauty.

Until books became widely available in sixteenth-century Europe, most stories were told through paintings, and most landscapes were created as backgrounds to religious art. Unlike his contemporaries, Joachim Patinir made the landscape the most important aspect of his work. In *Landscape with Saint Jerome* (page 11), the old **scholar** is the last thing we notice in this enormous painting.

Before science provided explanations for natural occurrences (such as thunder), the world was not only a place of beauty—it was also feared. In *View of Toledo* (page 19), El Greco painted a great storm and made people seem insignificant by comparison.

In the twentieth century, many artists have used the landscape as a way of expressing their love of the natural world. In *Grey Hills* (page 43), Georgia O'Keeffe portrayed mountains so ancient and removed from the world of mankind that they are like nature's monuments.

Artists transform what they see into images that take us to other times and places. You too can look from a great mountain or watch leaves fall in a forest and use your imagination to see like a painter.

Note: words in **bold** are explained in the glossary on pages 46–47.

GARDEN LANDSCAPE WITH BIRDS AND FOUNTAIN,
detail, 40–30 B.C.
Unknown Roman artist, **fresco**, about 180 cm high

Wealthy citizens of Ancient Rome escaped the stress of city life in their luxurious country villas. The Roman villa was a place to relax and entertain guests with vast banquets. The villa was often also a visual feast with interior walls covered in murals.

Painting the column

This garden seems so real, we feel that we could step past the column

*Even though the **perspective** is not realistic, the painted column is so realistic that we believe the illusion of the landscape.*

and sip water from the little fountain. The painter created an **illusion** of **realistic** space and light by framing the landscape with a *trompe l'oeil* column. *Trompe l'oeil* is a French term that means to 'trick the eye', usually into believing that an object painted on a flat surface is real. The artist painted a pattern of golden grapevines swirling around the column to give the appearance of a round, solid shape. On the left side of the column, the plants are repeated in a dark red to give an illusion of solidity. The **transparent** white **highlight** streaking from the top to the bottom completes the illusion.

The colours of illusion

The artist painted the landscape in colours that fool us. The cool, dark brown cave seems to fall back into the hill and the warm, golden rocks appear to push forward. The artist unified this simple **composition** by repeating the pattern of the leaves and vines everywhere.

LANDSCAPE WITH SAINT JEROME, detail, undated Joachim Patinir, Flemish (about 1480–1524), oil on board, 72.5 x 87.5 cm

Joachim Patinir completed his art training in 1515 in Antwerp, Belgium, a thriving city that attracted many painters. Patinir soon became known as the first European landscape specialist. As an **apprentice** Patinir created landscape backgrounds (the part of the painting behind the main subject) for other artists. When he was a master artist Patinir painted sweeping scenes that suggest the vastness of the Earth.

Using different viewpoints

Patinir imagined standing on top of a high mountain to create this view across fields, valleys, lakes and islands. By placing the line of the horizon (see **perspective**) near the top of the picture and varying his view of the landscape, Patinir gave the picture a feeling of depth. At

first, it seems that Patinir is looking down from a high viewpoint. But he painted the buildings, people, and animals as if they are seen from ground level. The change in the point of view allows us to see the variety of natural shapes and **architecture**.

Patinir only used four basic colours—green, blue, ochre (yellowish-white), and brown. By mixing shades of each colour, he unified everything — from the flowers in the foreground (front) to the castles in the distance.

To Patinir, human activity seemed unimportant compared with nature's huge size and variety.

VIEW OF ARCO, 1495
Albrecht Dürer, German (1471–1528), water-colour on paper,
20 x 20 cm

*A*lbrecht Dürer was a painter who was inspired by the printing press to bring knowledge to a great number of people. He became famous in his lifetime as an illustrator, editor, and printer of books.

Dürer expanded his artistic knowledge by travelling whenever he could leave his busy workshop. In Venice, Italy, he visited Andrea Mantegna (1430/1–1506) and Gentile Bellini (1429–1507) and saw their landscape paintings. Like Joachim Patinir, these artists created landscapes as backgrounds for their religious art. Because he enjoyed studying nature, Dürer began to create paintings in which the scenery became the main subject.

Albrecht Dürer painted this detailed water-colour in order to study natural forms and enrich the detail in his landscape paintings.

A tourist picture

On his journey from Venice to his home in Nuremberg, Dürer painted this view of a fortified mountain village. He framed the picture with greyish brown rocks. A curving road leads our eyes to Arco, but Dürer slows down our visual journey by painting the vineyards and olive groves in great detail.

Dürer mastered the art of perspective by adding **opaque** white paint to his cool transparent water-colours. In the background, he whitened the green and brown slopes to make the distance hazy. By balancing the strong colours and detail in the middle of the picture with the pale background, Dürer combined his studies of nature (above) with his personal vision of nature.

Benedict klawsen

13

THE ADORATION OF THE SHEPHERDS, about 1505–10
Giorgione da Castelfranco, Italian (1475/7–1510), 87.5 x 107 cm

Giorgione was inspired by the light in Castelfranco, the hill town where he was born. His observations of nature led him to invent a new painting method that was revolutionary at the time.

Painting without outlines

In the sixteenth century, artists were taught to make detailed drawings of every aspect of their subject before painting it. The use of colour was considered less important than an artist's ability to

*Giorgione made this nativity scene look like a **contemporary** event by setting it in the country-side where he had lived as a child.*

draw. But Giorgione worked in colour from the beginning. He had noticed that objects in nature do not have outlines and so created a feeling of light, air, and space by building up shades of colour without outlines.

Giorgione leads us on a circular walk into the landscape by painting curved and vertical shapes. He painted the lake as three flattened ovals that become smaller in size as they go into the background. A little path curves back from the shore towards the hillside beyond. The geometric lines of the golden tower, lakeside villa and ruined castle follow the circular path of Giorgione's design from the foreground to the horizon. With touches of red, Giorgione warmed the golden **tones** in the landscape to capture the beautiful light of the Venetian countryside.

HUNTERS IN THE SNOW, 1565
Pieter Brueghel, Flemish (1525/30–69), oil on panel, 115 x 158 cm

*a*t a time when most artists painted dreamy landscapes filled with heroic figures, Pieter Brueghel created pictures of ordinary Flemish people who made their living from the land. In this painting, one in a series depicting the four seasons, Brueghel captured the frozen world of winter in a scene that stretches for miles.

What can we see?

Three trees and three hunters with their pack of dogs lead our eye in a diagonal line to the jagged, distant mountains. The foreground is filled with steep-roofed cottages that guide our eyes down the snowy slope to the different activities below. We notice the bright red colour of an apron and two women skating on a frozen inlet of water. Our eye moves past a farmer carrying firewood across a little bridge, to the open fields beyond. Here, Brueghel divided the large pond into two smaller areas, with people fishing through the ice on one side and playing games on the other.

The colours of winter

To emphasize the bitter chill of winter, Brueghel painted a dull, greenish blue sky. The warm brick colour of the cottages and the fire make the day seem even colder.

Behind the village church, eight people with buckets and ladders attempt to put out a chimney fire.

VIEW OF TOLEDO, about 1597
El Greco (Doménikos Theotokópoulos), Spanish, born in Crete
(1541–1614), oil on canvas, 118.5 x 106 cm

The painter who became known as The Greek—El Greco, in Spanish—wandered from his native Crete to Venice, to Rome, and then to Madrid in search of a **patron** who would buy his paintings. In the capital of Spain, King Philip II rejected him as a court painter.

The ant-like textile workers washing cloth in the river makes the landscape seem overwhelming.

The king thought El Greco's colours were too harsh and his painting style too crude. Finally, in Toledo, Spain, the artist found a patron. El Greco became an official painter for the Catholic church in 1577 and lived in Toledo for the rest of his life.

A stormy landscape

This landscape painting was unusual for El Greco, who usually created religious paintings and portraits of church officials. El Greco captured the fury of a thunderstorm by exaggerating shapes and colours. He made the hill much steeper than it is in reality and perched the buildings precariously on top of the cliff. The black clouds are blown along by a fierce wind and the rocks and buildings seem to vibrate under the white light that turns the colour of the grass to acid green.

El Greco made the massive shapes of the sky and the land with bold brushstrokes. He then added highlights to the rocks, trees, and buildings. By changing the positions of Toledo's cathedral and castle, El Greco focuses our attention on the church—his loyal patron for forty years.

EVENING: LANDSCAPE WITH AN AQUEDUCT, detail,
1818 Théodore Géricault, French (1791–1824), oil, 246 x 215 cm

Théodore Géricault began his career as a painter during a grim period in France's history: **Napoleon** had been defeated, and Paris was occupied by Russian and British soldiers. Géricault often **symbolized** his country's difficulties by depicting people faced with the destructive power of nature. His images of shipwrecks and drownings make the viewer identify with the fear of the people in the paintings. In this huge landscape painting, more than two and a half metres high, Géricault achieved the same kind of gloomy effect.

A frightening landscape

Dangerously steep cliffs dominate the landscape. A ruined castle grows out of the hill. On top of a shadowy mountain we see the blank walls of a darkened tower. The **aqueduct** is like a barrier stopping us from seeing the lake beyond. Géricault stacked one rocky shape on top of another to create a fear-inspiring image.

Géricault painted the warm brown colours of the landscape and the architecture and then applied layers of grey paint that allow the reddish brown colour below to show through. By using a limited range of colours, he created the atmosphere of evening light. In his short life, Géricault's pictures of nature's power over people marked a change in a two-hundred-year-old French painting tradition.

In this detail, tiny figures climbing and swimming help us to realize the enormous height of the cliffs.

20

ROAD WITH CYPRESS AND STAR, 1890
Vincent van Gogh, Dutch (1853–90), oil on canvas, 90 x 71 cm

In nature, Vincent van Gogh found the inspiration for his art. Every time he picked up a brush, he expressed his desire to bring joy to the people who saw his paintings. Van Gogh described this painting in a letter to his friend, the artist Paul Gauguin (1848–1903):

> "I still have a cypress with a star from [**Provence**], a last attempt—a night sky with a moon without radiance, the slender crescent barely emerging from the opaque shadow cast by the earth—one star with an exaggerated brilliance, a soft brilliance of pink and green in the ultramarine sky, across which some clouds are hurrying. Below, a road bordered with tall yellow canes, an old inn with yellow lighted windows, and a very tall cypress, very straight, very sombre. Very romantic, if you like, but also 'Provence', I think."

Painting light and colour

Van Gogh captured the energy of life with his powerful brushwork, using paint as thick as toothpaste. Each brush mark stands up from the canvas, allowing the colours underneath to show through. Individual strokes of yellow ochre, orange, ultramarine, and green, on top of **cerulean** blue, form a night sky that vibrates with light. Van Gogh repeated the green colour that he used in the sky and in the cypress tree throughout—on the wavy surface of the road, among the flame-like stalks of cane, and on the little inn. With dashes of white paint, he lit the landscape with the ghostly light of an eclipse of the moon.

Vincent van Gogh's fragile mental health collapsed two months after he painted this landscape and he took his own life. He lives on in his art and in the moving letters he wrote to his family and friends.

THE BONAVENTURE PINE, 1893
Paul Signac, French (1863–1935), oil on canvas, 65 x 80 cm

Paul Signac became the spokesman for a group of painters that gathered around the French painter Georges Seurat (1859–91) in the 1880s. Seurat had found that two dots of colour side by side created the effect of a third colour. The paintings of Seurat and Signac, which were covered with millions of individual dabs of colour, inspired art critics to call their **technique 'pointillism'**.

A landscape of dots
Signac organized exhibitions and published illustrated books to promote the group's work. When Seurat died in 1891, Signac was depressed by the loss of his friend. He left Paris for a fishing village in the south of France, where the warm climate renewed his energy. Signac then took pointillism a step further by using larger dots in **contrasting** colours to capture the rich landscape of the south.

Pairs of colours
In this painting of a majestic pine tree, Signac used pairs of **complementary colours**—red and green, blue and orange, yellow and violet—in their brightest **hues**. With these sharply contrasting colours, Signac painted shadows and highlights that create the effect of sparkling southern light. For the leaves, he painted dabs of green and blue, adding spots of orange to define the edges. The light-dappled shadows in the foreground are made up of touches of violet and yellow paint. Signac saw that strong reflections off the water created a hazy light, which he captured by painting speckles of yellow over the water, sky, and distant hills.

Another great artist, Vincent van Gogh (see pages 22-3), had paired complementary colours. Signac's bold and deliberate use of colour gave French painting a new direction.

VIEW FROM MY WINDOW, ERGANY, 1888
Camille Pissarro, French (1830–1903), oil on canvas, 62 x 78 cm

In the 1870s, Camille Pissarro, the great landscape painter, became friend and adviser to Paul Cézanne (see pages 28-9) and Claude Monet (1840–1926). He encouraged these younger artists to pursue their ideas about painting, despite harsh public criticism. When Pissarro was fifty-five years old he met Georges Seurat and Paul Signac (see pages 24-5). Their new pointillist technique gave Pissarro a fresh source of energy for his work.

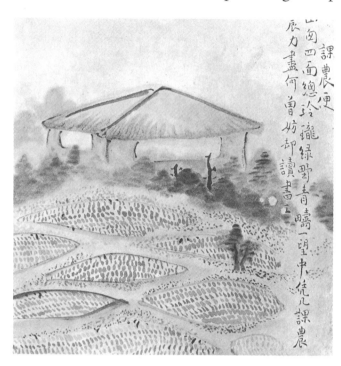

山田四面總玲瓏綠野青疇一望中

辰力盡何曾妨却讀書工

課農便

依几課農

Like many artists of his generation, Camille Pissarro appreciated Japanese landscape paintings. Ike No Taiga, who lived one hundred years earlier, suggested the fields in this painting with an **abstract** *pattern of brushstrokes.*

Dots of light
Like Signac and Seurat, Pissarro painted dots of colour. By placing two colours next to each other on the canvas, instead of mixing paint on the **palette**, he created the effect of a third colour. To the viewer, the colours seem to blend together. For example, dots of red and yellow look like orange when seen from a few metres away.

Wandering through the composition
Pissarro's composition keeps our eyes moving through the painting. The red barn roof points to the poplar trees in the background. A ring of fruit trees around the meadow brings us back to the greenhouse, the garden, and Mrs. Pissarro in the foreground.

BIBEMUS QUARRY, about 1895
Paul Cézanne, French (1839–1906), oil on canvas, 63.5 x 97.5 cm

*B*ecause he was interested in nature, Paul Cézanne went to the south of France. The way in which he painted light inspired younger artists, such as Henri Matisse (see pages 36-7) and André Derain (see pages 34-5), who searched for similar ways to express themselves.

In an abandoned quarry near Aix-en-Provence, Cézanne studied the huge, jagged rocks and made this dramatic composition by contrasting sizes, shapes, and angles.

A circular composition

Cézanne arranged the rock shapes in a pattern. Large stones on the left and right guide our eyes into the painting. The horizontal shelf in the middle leans towards a wedge-shaped outcrop that sweeps upward. Soft green plants creep up the slope to a tree on the horizon. The diagonal trunk of a tree cut off by the edge of the painting takes us back along sharply tilted rocks to the middle of the picture. The rocks below move our attention back into the painting.

Painting rocks and sky

Every stroke of Cézanne's brush makes the rocks look solid. He painted patches of red, brown, orange, and grey side by side and created weightless clouds in the hazy-looking sky with short brushstrokes, in many shades of grey and blue.

In this painting, Cézanne emphasized the steep landscape by contrasting light tones in the foreground with dark tones in the trees and sky.

BEECH FOREST I, 1902
Gustav Klimt, Austrian (1862–1918), oil on canvas, 97 x 97 cm

Gustav Klimt became a well-known painter at the age of twenty, when he was still a student. After joining the only official art organization in Vienna, Austria, he fought for freedom of expression. The organization was run by old-fashioned people who were more interested in selling works of art than in finding new ways of painting. In 1897, Klimt formed an art association that promoted new art through exhibitions and a monthly magazine.

Leaving the city

Important mural and portrait **commissions** as well as his work for the art association left Klimt with little spare time. But every autumn, he left Vienna for the lake district near Salzburg, where he experimented with new ideas by painting landscapes.

A painting like a tapestry

For this haunting forest scene, Klimt was inspired by a technique he had noted in Japanese art—he placed the line of the horizon close to the top of the painting to show its distance from the viewer. The bird's-eye view and pale grey colour in the background suggest depth. The multicoloured pattern of individual brush marks on the leaves and speckled tree trunks make the painting seem flat, like a tapestry. With speckles of brilliant gold sunlight that form a strong contrast to the grey and rust tones in the painting, Klimt created a decorative effect.

The year after Klimt painted this ghostly landscape, a mural he created for Vienna's new university was rejected by the head of the school, who thought it was obscene. After this, Klimt refused projects for public buildings and, instead, spent more of his time on landscape painting.

BANKS OF THE BIEVRE NEAR BICETRE, 1904
Henri Rousseau, French (1844–1910), oil on canvas, 53.5 x 45 cm

Before he became a full-time artist, Henri Rousseau worked as a clerk for the customs department, inspecting cargo on river barges in the Paris suburbs.

The tiny figures make the trees seem enormous by comparison. Rousseau was known for his jungle images and painted tropical leaves on these city trees.

A simple style

Rousseau was a self-taught artist who made copies of masterpieces in the Louvre museum in order to learn about art. At the museum, he developed his technical skills and sharpened his talent for using colour. Rousseau painted in a clear, simple style that he believed was the truest—and the best—expression of his feelings about nature.

A sense of depth

In this landscape, Rousseau created an illusion of depth by using angles to lead our eyes from the foreground into the background. Four paths, separated by grass, sweep back into the distance. A tiny family strolls down the wedge-shaped paths toward the little white house beyond.

Rousseau used a limited number of colours to capture the dream-like atmosphere of a hazy spring day. He repeated the green of the grass in the trees and made leaves by painting speckles of yellow ochre on the trees and hedges. Rousseau framed the scene with towering trees whose branches swirl in a spring breeze.

THE CYPRESSES, 1907
André Derain, French (1880–1954), oil on board, 23.5 x 32.5 cm

In this landscape painting, André Derain honoured two master artists who had influenced his work: Vincent van Gogh (see pages 22-3), and his powerful use of intense colours to express emotion, and Paul Cézanne (see pages 28-9), because of his many paintings of Mont Sainte-Victoire (below). In 1907, Derain spent the summer in the south of France where the two artists had painted. He adopted their themes—the cypress trees and the mountain—to create a painting that shows space and natural light in a different way.

Blocks of colour

With bold blocks of colour, Derain created an impression of depth. Wedge-shaped walls point into the distance. The road, framed by hedges, leads back towards the mountain. Tall greenish-black cypresses march into the background. The blue pyramid of Mont Sainte-Victoire is mirrored by a pale blue triangle of distant sky.

Coloured shadows

Derain noted that bright light cast shadows that were dark reflections of their subjects—not just black masses. He painted the shadows cast by the hedges in the foreground in pale lavender. The energy with which Derain painted Mont Sainte-Victoire can be seen in the lively brushstrokes that cover the surface of the painting.

Paul Cézanne took a distant view of Mont Sainte-Victoire in this oil painting. He drew the peak with patches of paint applied with a square brush .

MOROCCAN LANDSCAPE, 1912
Henri Matisse, French (1869–1954), oil on canvas, 116 x 78.5 cm

Like an athlete, Henri Matisse did a series of warm-up exercises before starting a large, important painting. Matisse made quick sketches to capture gestures or movements and drew long, detailed studies to compose the painting. As he drew, he made decisions about how he would use lines, colours, and shapes. When he began to paint, Matisse relied on his instincts and used colour to express emotions rather than just to describe the appearance of things.

Painting paradise

On a visit to Tangier, Morocco, in 1912, Matisse found an exotic country with gardens that delighted his senses. In this painting, Matisse simplified the forms and colours of the rich landscape into his dream of paradise.

Matisse drew many studies of acanthus leaves, memorizing their shape with both his eyes and his hands. When he painted the acanthus, he simplified the leaves to a pattern in the foreground of the picture. Matisse balanced the curved and flowing composition with one stately tree. This strong shape creates a striking contrast to the patterns of plants around it.

Painting heat

To imitate the warmth of Morocco, Matisse painted radiant pink over the entire canvas. He covered the foreground with blue paint to suggest shadows. Patches of pink show through the blue to show sunlight filtering through the trees. With touches of chrome yellow, Matisse made the picture look as though it is full of the heat of the sun.

THE RIDE OF PAUL REVERE, 1931
Grant Wood, American (1892–1942), oil, 75 x 100 cm

"The British are coming! The British are coming!"

Grant Wood was inspired by Paul Revere, the silversmith who warned his neighbours of the enemy's advance on Lexington and Concord during the American Revolution (1775–83). Wood believed that ordinary people were involved in important events, and he often drew the everyday life of the farmers in Iowa, where he lived. Wood moved Paul Revere's historic ride from Massachusetts, where it actually took place, to the American midwest, transforming the distant national figure into a hero of Wood's own region.

A stage set
This bird's-eye view makes the scene look like a stage set seen from high up in the balcony. Like a theatre director, Wood created an effect by pouring artificial-looking moonlight over the scene from above. He emphasized the church with a long, sharp shadow and cast an eerie neon green glow over the banks of the little stream. Wood painted the geometric shapes of the buildings very precisely.

Changing the landscape
Wood made New England resemble Iowa by emphasizing the rolling hills with a curving road. By placing the tiny horse and rider next to the tallest building, Wood draws attention to Paul Revere's lonely ride.

Wood admired the brushwork of Joachim Patinir's landscapes (detail from page 11).

RANDEGG IN THE SNOW, WITH RAVENS, 1935, Otto Dix, German (1891–1969), mixed media on board, 78.5 x 67.5 cm

When Adolf Hitler came to power in Germany in 1933, he forced artists to create romantic paintings that would glorify the crazed ideas of Nazi superiority. Otto Dix's paintings were fiercely critical of conditions in Germany and were labelled 'immoral'. He was sacked from his teaching job at the Dresden Academy and much of his work was destroyed by the Nazis. Fearing for his family's safety, Dix moved with them to the remote village of Randegg.

*Many twentieth-century painters were influenced by wood-block **prints** of the four seasons by the nineteenth-century Japanese artist Andō Hiroshige.*

A personal landscape

Although Dix refused to paint the kind of pictures demanded by Hitler, he had to sell his work in order to support his family. Like Brueghel (see pages 16-17), Dix painted a winter scene with a view from high up above a village. But Dix's landscape has a different mood from Brueghel's. Dix drew a world shut off from trouble. He warmed the cold light with a hidden sun but the gnarled tree and the black ravens suggest his sadness at his isolation from his friends in Dresden.

Borrowing from the past

The precision of Dix's brushwork resembles Albrecht Dürer's (see pages 12-13). With fine brushes, Dix painted every feather on the swooping ravens, every branch, and every icicle. Dix used the themes and techniques of past artists in order to create paintings that would sell during desperate times.

40

GREY HILLS, 1942, Georgia O'Keeffe, American (1887–1986), oil on canvas, 60 x 90 cm

On her first visit to New Mexico, in 1929, Georgia O'Keeffe was captivated by a desert landscape with dramatic skies and mountains of intense, unfamiliar colours. Nearly every year after 1929 she escaped the frantic pace of New York life to go to Ghost Ranch in a remote part of New Mexico.

Massive mountains

O'Keeffe often camped out in Navaho Indian territory, near a range of hills that she said looked like miles of elephants. Rising before dawn, O'Keeffe watched the ghostly moonlight light up the hills. Because there are no figures in this painting, we cannot 'measure' the mountain's height. By taking out the background and foreground, O'Keeffe made a close-up composition that crowds the viewer out of the scene.

Painting moonlight

To capture the ghostly quality of moonlight, O'Keeffe painted grey highlights that are not much brighter than the shadows. She drew the mountain's sides in warm colours that she made by mixing the earth colours of sand, yellow ochre and red with black and white.

The contemporary American artist Yuko Nii created a haunting picture of Egyptian pyramids in a painting so realistic that it could almost be mistaken for a photograph.

LYNX WOODS, 1947
Charles Burchfield, American (1893–1967), water-colour on paper laid down on board, 81 x 98.5 cm

From the time he was a child, Charles Burchfield took walks by himself in the forest. He noted the patterns of light and the shapes of windswept leaves; he smelled musty dried moss and listened to the sounds of forest animals. Burchfield often lay in the woods with his eyes closed in order to feel the energy of nature — he felt nature with all of his senses and even heard the sound of a falling leaf.

Winter is coming

In *Lynx Woods*, Burchfield captured the mood of late summer with boldly patterned colours and shapes. With yellow, grey, and umber paint, Burchfield drew a shower of falling leaves. A misty light in the background invites us into the woods. But dusk is approaching, winter is coming, and the forest will soon be dark and cold.

A new technique

Although he attended art school, Charles Burchfield was really a self-taught artist. Working alone, he invented a unique method of water-colour painting using transparent and opaque paints. With transparent yellow paint, he created streams of sunlight. Large areas of cool grey and umber make the yellow seem even more brilliant by contrast. On the tree trunks and on the ground, Burchfield created a pattern of yellow and grey wildcat markings.

Burchfield rarely travelled. He found everything he needed to inspire his personal view of nature in the forest near his home outside Albany, New York.

Glossary and Index

ABSTRACT: a picture or sculpture which has shape and colour but no recognizable subject.

APPRENTICE: a person who works for a master artist in exchange for artistic training such as preparing paints, mounting canvas on to frames, and cleaning the studio.

AQUEDUCT: a man-made channel for conveying water.

ARCHAEOLOGIST: someone who studies the past by digging for the objects and ruins of past civilizations.

ARCHITECTURE: either a building that has been carefully designed or the art of designing buildings.

CERULEAN: the name given to the colour dark sky-blue.

COLOUR: when it is used by painters three different terms are used for colour.

    The actual appearance of the colour (red, blue, bluish green, etc.) is called its **hue**.

    A lighter or darker version of a **hue** is created by adding white or black and is called a shade.

    A **hue** can be changed by adding a small amount of another colour and this is called a tint.

COMMISSION: a work of art produced for a **patron**.

COMPLEMENTARY COLOURS: colours that are the opposite of each other.

COMPOSITION: the arrangement of objects and figures in a painting and the combination of colours and shapes in the painting.

CONTEMPORARY: of the same period in time.

CONTRASTING: the differences in light and dark, shapes and colours.

FRESCO: the name given to a type of painting where the artist paints on to wet plaster instead of a canvas. The paint is part of the wall and dries with the plaster.

HIGHLIGHT: the lightest colour or brightest white in a painting.

HUE: the actual appearance of a colour.

ILLUSION: something which looks real but is not.

MURAL: a very large painting that decorates a wall or is created as part of a wall. *See also* FRESCO.

NAPOLEON: (1769-1821) in 1799 Napoleon overthrew the French government and made himself the ruler of France (1804-14 and 1814-15).

OPAQUE: something which does not let light pass through it. Opaque paints hide what is under them. (The opposite of TRANSPARENT.)

PALETTE: the name of the board that artists mix their paint on.

PATRON: an organization or individual who **commissions** artists and sculptors to work for him or her.

PERSPECTIVE: a method of drawing people, places, and things to make them appear solid or three-dimensional rather than flat. Six basic rules of perspective are used in Western art.

1. People in a painting appear larger when they are near to the viewer and gradually become smaller as they get further away.
2. People in the foreground overlap the people or objects behind them.
3. People get closer together as they get further away.
4. People in the distance are closer to the top of the picture than those in the foreground.
5. Colours are brighter and shadows are stronger in the foreground. Colours and shadows are paler and softer in the background.
6. Lines that, in real life, are parallel (such as the line of a ceiling and the line of a floor) are drawn at an angle, and the lines meet at the horizon line, which is the line that represents the eye level of the artist and the viewer.

POINTILLISM: to paint with individual dots of colour rather than brushstrokes.

PRINT: an image created by a machine. Prints can be made from a metal plate (etching, aquatint, engraving), from a block of wood (wood engraving, wood-block print), from a silk gauze (silk-screen print), or from a stone (lithograph).

PROVENCE: the name of an area in the south of France.

REALISTIC: something which looks real.

SCHOLAR: an expert in a field of learning.

SYMBOLIZED: an image that represents something other than itself.

TECHNIQUE: the process or practice that is used to obtain a particular artistic effect.

TONE: the overall colour of a painting. For example, an artist might begin by painting the entire picture in shades of greenish grey. After more colours are added using **transparent** shadows and highlights, the mass of greenish grey colour underneath will show through and create an even tone. *See also* COLOUR.

TRANSPARENT: something which allows light to pass through it. A transparent colour allows colours underneath it to be seen. (The opposite of OPAQUE.)

TROMPE L'OEIL: the name given to the **technique** where an artist paints a scene so realistically that the viewer is tricked into thinking that the people and objects in the picture are real. *See also* PERSPECTIVE.

Credits